DISCOVER

OCEAN LIFE

Writer:
Alice Jablonsky

Consultant:
Steven Webster

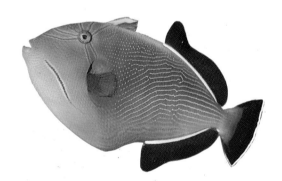

pil

Publications International, Ltd.

Manufactured in China.

8 7 6 5 4 3 2 1

ISBN: 0-7853-6111-1

Photo Credits:

Animals Animals: 13; G.I. Bernard: 41; M.A. Chappell: 24; E.R. Degginger: 26; Steve Earley: 25; Ashod Frances: K. Gillett: 30; Richard Kolar: 13; Zig Leszczynski: 24, 39, 42; C.C. Lockwood: 16; Oxford Scientific Films: 32; Peter Parks: 32; Tim Rock: 41; Carl Roessler: 24, 28; Dr. Nigel Smith: 13; Lewis Trusty: 25, 40; James D. Watt: 31; Anne Wertheim: 23; Joyce Wilson: 12; **Getty Images:** Endsheets & Back cover; FPG International: 1, 8; F. Cooler: 10; Jeff Divine: 5; John E. Gorman: 18, 42; Farrell Grehan: 12; Michael S. Kass: 20; Keystone View Company: 6; Bill Losh: 9; Buddy Mays: 31; Carl Roessler: 29, 41; H. Ross: 42; K. Rothman: 10; Herbert Schwarte: 14, 15; The Telegraph Colour Library: 4; John Turner: 22; **International Stock:** George Ancona: 24, 26, 28; Dennis Fisher: 22; Tom & Michele Grimm: 12; Steven Lucas: 16; Maratea: 13; Seapics.com: Doug Perrine: Front and back cover; James D. Watt: 30; **Marty Snyderman:** 3, 11, 12, 14, 19, 20, 21, 23, 25, 26, 27, 29, 30, 31, 36, 37, 38, 39, 40, 42, 43; **Tom Stack & Associates:** 7, 8; Matt Bradley: 8; Paulette Brunner: 11, 28; John Caucalosi: 20; M. Hall Clason: 6; Dave B. Fleetham: 3, 7, 16, 18, 30; Jeff Foott: 22; Larry Lipsky: 14, 39, 41; Joe McDonald: 10; Bob McKeever: 6; Gary Milburn: 19, 43; M. Timothy O'Keefe: 17; Brian Parker: 11, 12, 16, 23, 24, 25, 36, 43; Edward Robinson: 14, 29, 43; Kevin Schafer: 8; Dennis Tackett: 38; F. Stuart Westmorland: 10, 36; Anna E. Zuckerman: 6; **Norbert Wu:** 3, 32, 33, 34, 35, 40.

Illustrations: Pablo Montes O'Neill; Lorie Robare

Alice Jablonsky spent childhood vacations along the Atlantic shore, where she learned to love the sea. As a senior researcher and writer at the National Geographic Society, she contributed to many of their publications for adults and children, including *America's Seashore Wonderlands, Majestic Island Worlds, Whales: Might Giants of the Sea,* and *Explore a Rocky Shore.* As a certified scuba diver, Ms. Jablonsky's explorations have taken her from the Caribbean Sea to the Indian Ocean.

Steven Webster is the Director of Education for the world-famous Monterey Bay Aquarium. He obtained his degree in biological sciences from Stanford University and has taught invertebrate zoology and marine biology courses for divers in the Caribbean on Grand Cayman and St. Croix islands. He was honored as an Educator of the Year by the Sierra Club in 1989, and his underwater photographs have appeared in numerous publications.

CONTENTS

OUR BIG, BLUE PLANET

If you could view the earth from outer space, you would see a beautiful blue planet. The blue color is water, which covers more than 70 percent of the earth's surface. Most of this is salty ocean water. Water makes life possible, and, because other planets don't have any, earth is different from all the other planets in the solar system.

Maps and globes show oceans with separate names. It is important to remember that the ocean is really one large body of water. The continents on which we live are simply large islands set in the ocean. We divide the ocean waters using natural boundaries created by land. We usually call the larger bodies of water "oceans" and the smaller ones "seas."

The largest ocean is the Pacific, which holds thousands of tropical islands, including the Hawaiian Islands. The waters of the Atlantic separate the continents of North and South America from Europe and Africa. The Indian Ocean is the smallest ocean; it lies between Africa and Australia.

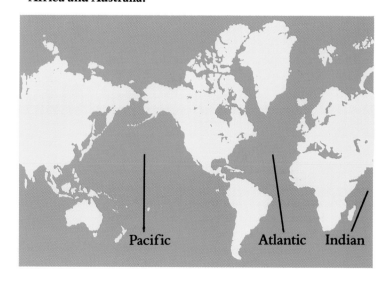

Pacific   Atlantic   Indian

Water makes life possible on this planet. No other planet in our solar system has water or life.

Arctic and Antarctic Oceans may seem too cold for life. But these freezing waters are teeming with fish and are home to whales and other sea mammals.

Ocean water—all water, really—"recycles" itself. It evaporates and rises into the sky to become clouds. When a cloud becomes heavy with moisture, rain falls.

Early explorers depended upon the oceans and seas for travel and trade. Sailors must have wondered what sorts of creatures lived in the  waters below their ships. It has been only in the last 100 years that modern science has studied ocean life.

The largest of the oceans is the Pacific. Its waters separate North and South America from Asia and Australia. Thousands of islands are scattered over the warm, tropical Pacific Ocean. Many of these islands were formed thousands of years ago when volcanoes erupted beneath the surface of the water.

The Atlantic is the second largest of the oceans. It separates North and South America from Europe and Africa. A huge underwater mountain chain, called the Mid-Atlantic Ridge, curves along the ocean floor in the middle of the ocean.

Between Africa and Australia lies the smallest of the three major oceans—the Indian Ocean. It stretches around the shores of Saudi Arabia to the Persian Gulf and the Red Sea. Early European explorers made long voyages across the tropical Indian Ocean to buy silks and spices in India and China.

If you were to travel to the poles, you would see islands of ice floating on the Arctic and Antarctic waters. Fewer kinds of animals and plants live in the polar seas than in the tropics. But the creatures that do live there are often found in great numbers.

Where did all of this water come from? Oceans had their beginnings when the earth was new. Moisture was inside the earth when the planet was formed nearly five billion years ago. Volcanoes released the moisture from deep inside the forming earth. This produced great amounts of steam, lava, and other rocks. The earth's atmosphere was hot—so hot that all of the moisture that escaped turned into steam.

Over billions of years, the planet cooled. Cooler temperatures changed the steam to rain. Rain started to fill the deep canyons of the bare earth. The first rains were salty, as the rain was rich in minerals. Most of the ocean's salt today is from the first volcanic eruptions. Water evaporates and collects in the atmosphere only to fall again and again over the land as rain or snow. Again and again it flows to the ocean, carrying both minerals and chemicals—good and bad.

The floor of the ocean is much like the land on which we live. If you were to walk down a sandy beach into the ocean, you would feel the land gradually slope down, down, down. This rim of sloping underwater land is called the continental shelf. It is called this because it lies like a shelf at the edge of the continents.

Beyond the continental shelf, the ocean bed drops more steeply to much greater depths. Beyond this drop-off, parts of the floor are flat and are covered with mud, sand, silt, and the remains of dead plants and animals. But there are also mountains, valleys, and canyons beneath the sea. Some underwater mountains reach high enough above the water to form islands. Other islands are formed by volcanoes that reach above the water's surface.

The ocean averages 2.5 miles deep. That does not mean that ½ of it is at that depth. The deepest parts of the ocean, called trenches, are nearly seven miles deep! Some ocean mountain ranges are higher than the highest mountains on land!

The earth's first water was made of volcanic steam that cooled and turned into rain.

The first rains were salty. All the water that ran over the earth was salt water.

If the ocean were drained of its water, we'd see steep drop-offs, like cliffs, just beyond the edges of the continents.

7

THE EDGE OF THE OCEAN

is a strange place. It is both land and water, dry and wet. Every piece of land, from the largest continent to the smallest island, has a shore. Yet no two shorelines are quite the same.

Most people in the world live within 60 miles of a coast. If you have lived along a coast or spent summer vacations at the seashore, you probably have a favorite place to explore. Perhaps you like to look for

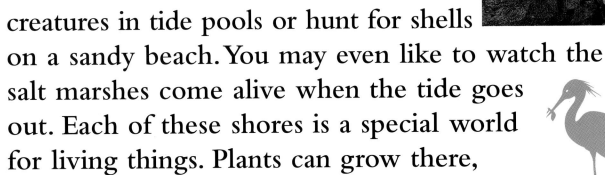

creatures in tide pools or hunt for shells on a sandy beach. You may even like to watch the salt marshes come alive when the tide goes out. Each of these shores is a special world for living things. Plants can grow there, bathed in the sunlit shallow waters. The rocks, sand, and grass beds are perfect hiding places where sea animals can grow, feed, and reproduce, safe from enemies.

8

THE EDGE OF THE OCEAN

Waves never stop crashing against the rocky shore. Animals and plants that live there have developed ways to survive the pounding surf.

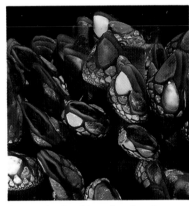

A crab (left) can skitter about the rocks looking for food. Its shell will keep it from being hurt if it is dashed against the rocks by a wave. These gooseneck barnacles (right) are "glued" to the rocks. Pulling their soft bodies inside their shells, they are quite safe from harm.

A sea star might lose an arm as it is tossed by the waves. It can grow a new one, though!

ROCKY SHORE

The rocky shore is home to the largest variety and the greatest number of seashore creatures. Animals occupy every available space. They are on the rocks, under rocks, and in cracks and holes. Animals even live under seaweeds and on the shells of other animals.

All rocky-shore plants and animals must survive the constant pounding of the surf. Animals like limpets and crabs wear hard shells for protection. Others seek a hole or other spots where the surf will not disturb them. To keep from being swept away by the waves, many creatures have ways of clinging to the rocks. A snail's foot lets it move slowly over the rocks or hold fast to one place. Barnacles fasten themselves to the rocks with "cement" they make with their bodies. Mussels attach themselves to rocks with tough, leathery threads. Sea stars have rows of tiny tube feet with suction cups at the tips. The sea star can move around on the rocks as well as cling tightly to the rocks during wave surges.

Some seaweed anchor themselves down with strong bases called holdfasts. When the tide goes out, the seaweed stays put. Have you walked over slippery blades of seaweed? Seaweed is slippery because of a coating that helps them hold in moisture and keep from drying out during low tides.

Tide pools are wonderful places to look for living things when you are exploring a rocky shore. A tide pool is a small pool of water left standing when the tide goes out. It shelters plants and animals that cannot live in the open air during low tides. Every tide pool contains a community of plants and animals. Some are bottom-dwellers, some attach themselves to the rocks, and others swim freely.

Seaweeds clinging to the rocks provide food and shelter for tidepool creatures. Small animals like hermit crabs often creep under the fronds for protection from the sun and wind. Hermit crabs do not have shells of their own. They live in shells left by snails.

Sea stars are related to sea urchins. Sea stars usually have five leathery arms. But some have as many as 45 arms!

If you look carefully into a tide pool, you will probably notice colorful "blossoms" clinging to the rocks. They may look like flowers, but they are really animals called sea anemones.

If you see a creature in a tide pool that looks like a giant pin cushion, it is probably a sea urchin. A sea urchin wears effective armor to protect it against enemies: Sharp spines cover its body.

A sea star eats mollusks. It uses the suckers on its tube feet to pull apart the shells. The star pushes its stomach out of its body through its mouth (above). The chemicals in its stomach will digest the fleshy animal inside the shell.

The urchin's mouth is on its underside. It has five sharp teeth that are strong enough to bite into tough algae, seaweeds, and coral.

When the hermit crab outgrows its shell, it simply moves into a larger one left behind by a snail.

Sea anemones have soft, stinging tentacles. As water flows over the anemones, they wave their tentacles to catch food floating by. When the tide goes out, anemones will pull in their tentacles so they do not dry out.

11

THE EDGE OF THE OCEAN

Pale ghost crabs (left) dig deep holes in the sand for protection. They must visit the sea often to get water, though. Horseshoe crabs (right) are not really crabs, but are related to spiders! They, too, burrow in the sand for protection. Ghost crabs are scavengers/predators. They don't feed by burrowing. They get protection by burrowing.

Dune grasses help form the sand dunes that protect coastlines from strong winds and high waters.

The bleached sand dollar you find washed up on the beach is the skeleton of an animal that is related to the sea urchin.

SANDY BEACH

You might think that few animals could live on a sandy beach. But many creatures find a home or a meal there. Some live in the sand at the edge of the beach. Some feed where the waves move back and forth. Others build nests in the sand dunes. Birds circle overhead, looking for food.

There are very few rocks to trap seaweeds along a sandy beach. But small animals still must protect themselves from the sun and waves. Most creatures seek shelter while the sand is very hot. They stay underground where it is damp and cool. Millions of tiny animals live in the water that collects between the grains of sand. Larger creatures also burrow in the sand. They move about in the early morning, late afternoon, at night, and at high tide.

Many kinds of crabs live near a sandy beach. Some, like sand crabs, are only an inch long. A sand crab catches food with its feather-shaped antennae. If you are careful, you might see ghost crabs walking along the beach. They seem to appear from nowhere, run quickly, and suddenly disappear.

As the surf splashes in, sanderlings race across the wet sand. These small birds try to catch shellfish that wash up in the waves. When the tide goes out, other birds such as gulls and sandpipers probe and dig along the shore.

12

SALT MARSH

A salt marsh is protected from the open sea by thick grasses and land. Seawater floods the marsh at high tide. At low tide, there is a lot to see on the muddy bottom of the marsh.

A waxy-looking plant called glasswort anchors itself in the squishy mud. While the tide is out, mussels lie on the mud. Their strong threads are attached to the grass. A mussel will open its shell to feed when the tide comes in. When the tide goes out, it closes its shell to keep from drying out.

Fiddler crabs find food in the mud at low tide. When the water rises, they race into their holes. Male fiddler crabs show off for females by waving their large claws.

The salt marsh has food for many creatures. Most animals live near the surface or in tubes or shallow burrows. Small animals may become meals for larger animals. Snowy egrets catch fish. Clapper rails eat fiddler crabs, snails, insects, and seeds.

Salt marshes are sometimes claimed by humans as building sites. This upsets the balance of nature, though, leaving many animals without food and shelter.

Salt marshes are great hunting grounds for birds like herons and egrets.

Heron

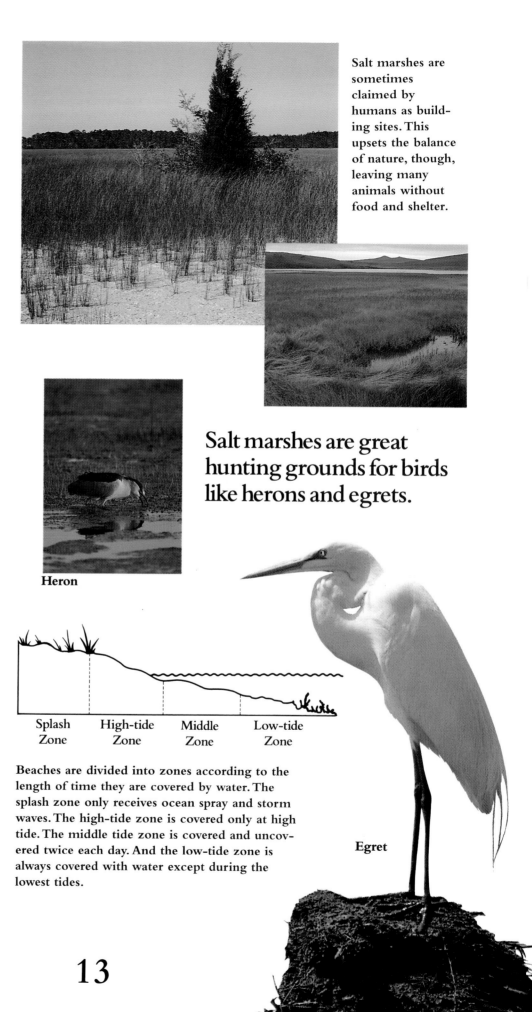

Splash Zone | High-tide Zone | Middle Zone | Low-tide Zone

Beaches are divided into zones according to the length of time they are covered by water. The splash zone only receives ocean spray and storm waves. The high-tide zone is covered only at high tide. The middle tide zone is covered and uncovered twice each day. And the low-tide zone is always covered with water except during the lowest tides.

Egret

CORAL REEFS

can be found only in certain places. The water must be clear and warm. Coral reefs grow in shallow waters of tropical oceans where there is plenty of sunlight.

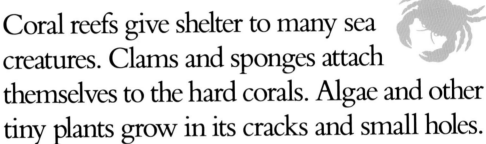

Coral reefs give shelter to many sea creatures. Clams and sponges attach themselves to the hard corals. Algae and other tiny plants grow in its cracks and small holes. Worms, crabs, and many kinds of fish move in and out of holes. Octopuses and eels find hiding places in larger caves.

Colorful fish sparkle like jewels as they dart in and out of the corals.

Coral reefs are important to people, too. Besides being a pleasure to explore by snorkeling and scuba-diving, reefs help protect some shorelines from the force of hard-hitting storm waves.

A living coral colony is made up of thousands of tiny animals called polyps. Most coral polyps measure less than an inch across, yet they create some of the largest things on earth—whole islands and reefs.

A reef begins when the egg of a coral hatches into a larva. This larva drifts with the waves and currents until it settles onto a hard surface. When the coral larva is three weeks old, it becomes a polyp. These polyps divide and form more polyps. Together, the polyps can build huge coral colonies. Some colonies grow to be the size of a car.

If you look closely at a coral skeleton, you will see tiny holes. Each hole is where a coral animal lived. A polyp is like a sac that is closed at one end and has a mouth at the other. Its mouth is surrounded

After it has anchored itself to a firm surface, a coral polyp builds a skeleton beneath its soft body. The skeleton is cup-shaped. A ship that has wrecked and sunk in warm shallow waters is the perfect place to begin a coral colony.

As new polyps keep building on old skeletons, they form a huge mass that becomes the base of a coral reef. This is Australia's Great Barrier Reef.

The coral skeleton is very hard, but the thin layer of living tissue is easily damaged.

by tentacles. These tentacles sting tiny sea creatures as they float by. Once stung, the prey is drawn into the polyp for food. The food on which a polyp feeds is the plankton that drifts with the ocean currents. During the day, most coral polyps stay collapsed with their tentacles drawn in. At night, they wave their tentacles to catch food.

Corals have tiny algae living inside them. The algae are single cells, and you would need a microscope to see them. Scientists have learned that the algae supply food for the coral and help the coral build its limestone skeleton.

There are more than 2,000 different kinds of corals. Some are hard and some are soft. Corals come in many colors—some are pink, some are deep red. Others are violet. Most are yellow-brown due to the algae in their tissues. When photographed underwater with a flash, the colors of corals appear even brighter. The brightly colored corals are not usually the reef builders.

Soft corals have tiny polyps that form branching tentacles that extend into the water. Sea fans are a kind of soft coral. They don't build reefs, though. Instead, their colonies wave gently with the movement of the water, like trees swaying in a breeze. Because sea fans bend, they rarely break when a storm stirs up the water. In some places they even form a protective barrier in front of a reef.

The most brightly colored corals are usually the soft corals. Hard corals are often a dull yellow-brown.

Stony corals, like this staghorn coral, can form huge underwater forests.

Sea fans are a type of soft coral. They do not build reefs, but they may help protect reefs from storm waves.

17

CORAL REEFS

If small fish swim together in a school, they may confuse an enemy and make it think they are really one big fish.

The brilliant colors and patterns worn by reef fish help them blend with their coral habitat.

Parrotfish have teeth that look like the tip of a parrot's beak. The parrotfish uses its "beak" to graze on algae and coral. Divers may hear a faint crunching sound if a school of parrotfish is grazing nearby.

Divers know never to reach inside a hole in a coral reef—a moray eel has strong jaws and sharp teeth!

Many fish that live near a coral reef are brightly colored. They flash and shimmer in the shallow waters. Their fancy colors and patterns may help the fish survive by hiding them from enemies. Some fish blend with the colors and patterns of the coral reef. Others wear "warning" colors. For instance, the stripes of the lion fish warn other fish to keep away.

Other fish have poisonous spines to protect them from enemies. The porcupine fish not only has spines but it also has another trick that can scare enemies away. The porcupine fish, and its relative, the pufferfish, can blow themselves up like balloons by swallowing water. By changing into a bigger fish, they might scare away a hungry enemy!

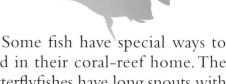

Some fish have special ways to feed in their coral-reef home. The butterflyfishes have long snouts with which to reach into cracks and holes for food.

The moray eel is a fish that looks like a snake. It has a long, muscular body and narrow jaws with sharp teeth. Some moray eels may grow to be ten feet long! The eel looks threatening as it opens and closes its mouth to breathe, passing water over its gills.

A moray eel is more likely to hide in a hole than to swim freely about the reef during the day. At night, however, the eel leaves its cave to search for prey. It feeds on crabs, small octopuses, and a variety of fish.

The octopus is another reef creature that prefers to stay hidden during the day. Like the eel, the octopus will creep out of its cave after dark to look for food. It travels across the ocean floor using its eight long arms. An octopus might be two to three feet long from its head to the tips of its arms. Others are small enough to be found in tide pools along a rocky shore. And a few octopuses can be as much as 14 feet long, but these are not found in the tropics.

An octopus can escape danger several different ways. It can change its color to blend with its surroundings. It can blast off like a rocket by forcing water very quickly from its grill chamber. It can also "disappear" before an enemy's eyes by squeezing its boneless body into a tiny hiding place. But the most famous trick of the octopus is to squirt an inky liquid from its body. By the time the water clears, the octopus will be gone!

Most people think of sponges as dried plants that are handy for washing the car or for taking a bath. But sponges are really sea animals. Sponges can be as small as a bean or as big as a car. Long, tubular sponges can grow to be six feet high. Others look like giant flower vases. Shrimp and small fish may make their homes in the holes of a sponge. Some sponges produce a chemical that eats away coral to "dig" a pit for itself where it may live undisturbed.

Suction cups on the undersides of its arms help the octopus cling to the reef. They also help it catch and pull apart its food. This octopus is eating a crab.

Some reef creatures like sponges, featherduster worms, and anemones look more like plants than animals.

A sponge pumps many gallons of water through its body every day. Tiny particles in the water are digested as they are pumped through hollow tubes in the sponge's body.

19

THE OCEAN HAS FORESTS

that are made up of plants called giant kelp. Kelp is one of thousands of kinds of seaweed.

Giant kelp grows in large beds in the cold waters along the coasts of California, Australia, New Zealand, and South America. Its long ribbons bob and sway in the endless roll of Pacific Ocean waves. Giant kelp can grow to be 200 feet long, which makes it the longest seaweed in the world. It can grow as much as two feet in a day!

Large kelp beds have much to offer fish and other marine animals. Fish hide and breed among its fronds. To keep from drifting away, sea otters wrap themselves in kelp while they sleep.

A sea otter must take very good care of its fur. Dirty fur does not hold in warmth; a cold otter will probably die.

Playful sea otters are right at home in the tangled fronds of giant kelp.

Before a sea otter goes to sleep in its kelp bed, it wraps itself in fronds to keep from drifting away (above). At mealtime, an otter will often use a rock to help it crack open the shellfish it has found (left).

Sea otters have adapted well to ocean life—and to life in a kelp bed, especially. They are good swimmers, having webbed toes on their hind feet. Otters often swim on their backs. To sleep and eat, the sea otter stretches on its back and wraps itself with kelp to keep from drifting away.

A sea otter has a very thick fur coat that keeps it dry and warm. The fur traps little pockets of air that help hold in body heat. If the fur gets too dirty, it will not hold in the air and the fur will soak up water. The otter will get wet and catch a chill. An otter with a chill will probably die. Therefore, sea otters spend several hours a day caring for their fur. This is called "grooming." The otter rolls over and over in the water to rinse food from its coat. It also cleans its fur by rubbing it with its front paws. Water is removed by licking, squeezing, and rubbing the fur.

Sea otters like to eat the soft meat of clams, abalones, crabs, fish, and sea urchins. An otter usually finds food in shallow water, but sometimes it dives nearly 200 feet to look for food. The otter stays underwater for about a minute while it collects shellfish to eat.

A sea otter may come to the surface with a rock as well as food. It uses the rock as a tool to open shells of the clams and urchins it gathers. The otter floats on its back with the rock on its chest. If the shellfish is hard to open, the otter smashes it on the rock.

The otter eats nearly a fourth of its weight in food every day. California fishermen blame sea otters for eating too much abalone, which brings a high price on the seafood market. In one day, a sea otter can eat 12 abalones, 20 sea urchins, 11 rock crabs, 60 kelp crabs, and 112 snails!

Sea otter mothers and babies—called "pups"—stay together for seven to nine months. The mothers teach their pups how to swim, to hunt for food, and to use rocks as tools.

Sea urchins look like living pincushions. Sometimes they live in large groups that form a prickly carpet on the sea floor. The urchin's mouth is on the underside of its body. It has five teeth that can crush small animals, chew plants, and scrape algae from rocks. The urchin often swallows large grains of sand when it eats. It grinds up the sand and sifts out the tiny bits of food. Then it spits out the sand in much smaller grains.

Urchins chew on kelp fronds that settle on the ocean floor; they also eat the holdfasts that anchor the kelp. Too many grazing urchins can destroy a kelp forest. Urchins are a favorite food of sea otters. Some people believe that sea otters help protect kelp forests by eating large numbers of urchins.

Kelp snail

Snails, limpets, and urchins graze on giant kelp. Too many grazers can harm a kelp bed.

How can anything eat such a prickly creature? Usually, a predator will turn the urchin over and attack its unprotected underside. Otters, however, have tough skin. The spines of the purple urchin (right) do not bother them.

Sea urchins eat not only fallen fronds of kelp, they also eat the holdfasts that anchor the kelp to the ocean floor. A colony of grazing urchins can destroy a giant kelp bed by cutting the kelp loose so that it drifts away.

The outside of an abalone's shell camouflages it against the ocean floor. The inside of the shell (right) is lined with "mother-of-pearl," which is often used in jewelry.

This luna clam (left) and oyster (right) are examples of "bivalves." "Bivalve" means "two valves," or "two shells." The clam has opened to catch food as it floats by.

Colorful nudibranchs are sometimes called the "butterflies of the sea."

"Mollusk" is the correct name for "shellfish" like clams, oysters, and abalone. Some mollusks are experts at clinging to rocks and seaweed. Some, like limpets and abalone, wear a hard shell like the snails they are. They move around on a sticky muscular foot. Limpets scrape the seaweed, eating any tiny plants and animals that are attached to the fronds. Limpets cling so tightly to a surface that they can be removed only if taken by surprise.

The shell of the abalone is rough and saucer-shaped. Like the limpet, the abalone moves along the ocean floor on its big muscular foot. It scrapes algae off rocks and grazes on kelp. When it senses danger, it uses its foot to clamp to a rock with great force.

Abalones are known for the beautiful pearly colors on the inside of their shells. Many people—as well as sea otters—find the animal inside quite tasty. Today, however, abalones are becoming rare. Too many have been harvested by humans and otters alike.

Nudibranchs are sea snails without shells. They glide along the sea floor among the kelp fronds, sponges, and anemones. Many nudibranchs are brightly colored. Their color is a warning to other sea creatures to stay away. Many nudibranchs are poisonous, sting, or taste bad.

People who dive in a kelp forest often come nose to nose with many kinds of fish. The garibaldi is a brilliantly colored fish. It can be scarlet red or golden yellow —or any shade in between! Garibaldi fish often lay their eggs among the rocks beneath the kelp.

The garibaldi's brilliant color is a warning to other fish to stay away.

The male garibaldi prepares the nest by first cleaning the algae off a rock. Then he allows certain kinds of algae to grow back. After the female lays her eggs on this algae, the male chases her off. He protects the eggs until the young hatch. Garibaldi fish are fierce guardians of their nests. They may even nip at scuba divers who swim too close.

Rockfish (left) and sheephead (right) are just two of the many fish that live in the cold waters of a kelp bed.

The giant sea bass glides through the kelp. It feeds on small fish and crabs that swim and crawl around the holdfasts of the kelp. The giant sea bass is a big fish—it can grow to be the size of a bathtub!

If you were to scuba dive in a kelp forest, you might see sea lions playing among the ribbons of seaweed. Sea lions belong to the group of sea mammals called pinnipeds. They spend part of their lives in the water and part on shore.

Sea lions swim among the ribbons of kelp, hunting for fish like the ones pictured above.

Like the otter, sea lions are also suited to life in the sea. A layer of blubber just under the skin keeps it warm and stores energy. The sea lion's shape is streamlined, which helps it move through the water with ease and speed. Flippers also help them swim and steer. Sea lions are like acrobats in a circus!

THE OPEN OCEAN

was feared by ancient sailors. They were afraid of sailing off the edge of the world and of being eaten by giant serpents. And what would happen if they were caught in terrible storms or were lost without sight of land?

Now we know more about the open sea where the sky and sea seem one. The open ocean is where hurricanes are born, swirling and whipping across the vast waters. We also know that under-

water earthquakes send tidal waves, called *tsunamis,* rolling for miles until they reach, and destroy, a shore. Some of the most fearsome animals are found in the open ocean. The great white shark and the Portuguese man-of-war both frighten and fascinate us. The open ocean is still a wilderness to humans.

Beachcombers should always be on the look-out for jellyfish—especially the Portuguese man-of-war (right)—that may have washed onto the shore. As long as the animal is alive, it can sting you.

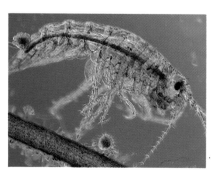

Plankton can be any kind of drifting animal or plant. The beach plea pictured above—and shown many times larger than its real size—may become food for a small fish, like an anchovy (right). These creatures are near the beginning of the ocean food chain.

Sailfish, swordfish, and some tuna can swim in bursts of speeds up to 70 miles per hour!

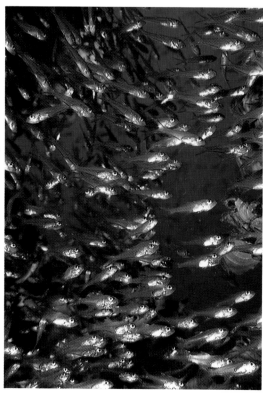

Away from land, the ocean is almost always clear. The muddy bottom of the ocean is far, far away. Also, there is less plankton to cloud the water. No rivers are near to stir up mud and sand, either.

At the surface of the open ocean are drifters. The giant yellow jellyfish and Portuguese man-of-war dangle their long, deadly tentacles under their soft bodies. Because they drift, they are considered plankton—plankton means "wanderer." Other plankton drift in these sunlit waters, too. Schools of small fish, like herring and anchovies, feed here on the tiniest plankton. These small fish become food for larger fish, like mackerel and bluefish. In turn, these are eaten by sharks and other big fish.

The fish that swim the open ocean have bodies designed to help them move fast through the water. Their bodies are sleek and slippery. Many fish are long and narrow. Their tails sweep from side to side, thrusting their bodies through the water. Fins balance the fish and help it steer.

Fins also help one kind of fish soar through the air! Flying fish can soar above the water on their "wing" fins. First, the fish must swim very fast. When they near the speed of 30 miles per hour, they launch their bodies into the air and catch the wind. Flying fish "fly" to escape from enemies.

Sharks must be perfect for life in the sea. Sharks have long, torpedo-shaped bodies. Their mouths are filled with rows and rows of razor-sharp teeth. They have a keen sense of smell and can also sense the movement of other animals in the water. All these things make sharks expert hunters.

A shark's mouth is a thing of wonder. When attacking, the shark's jaws actually move out of its mouth to open wide. Its lower jaw hits first; the upper jaw then snaps down with enough power to bite through a large seal. The shark's teeth lie row upon row, like shingles on a roof. As the front teeth are lost or worn out, the next row of teeth move up to take their place. Sharks never lose all their teeth.

The great white shark is the shark most feared by humans. A great white shark may grow to be 21 feet long and weigh nearly four tons. The teeth of a great white grow to be two inches long. The great white shark will eat just about anything.

Except for the great whales, the basking shark and the whale shark are the largest animals in the sea. They are larger, longer, and heavier than the great white shark. The basking shark can grow to be more than 30 feet long. It got its name because it prefers to bask in the sun, quietly floating on the surface of the water.

The great white shark (above) will sometimes attack humans. But this is probably because the shark has mistaken the person for its favorite food—the sea lion.

Shark skin is rough like sandpaper. A shark that brushes against you can cause a painful injury.

In spite of its size, which may be 50 feet or longer, the whale shark (right) is a peaceful giant. It feeds only on plankton and small fish.

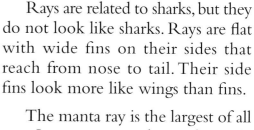

Rays are related to sharks, but they do not look like sharks. Rays are flat with wide fins on their sides that reach from nose to tail. Their side fins look more like wings than fins.

The manta ray is the largest of all rays. It may grow to be 22 feet, side to side; it may weigh more than a ton! It has two curved bumps on its head that look like horns. It's easy to see how it earned its nickname of "devilfish."

One of the largest reptiles in the sea is the marine turtle. Some sea turtles weigh as much as 700 pounds. They are found in the warm Gulf Stream off the East Coast. They also live in warm seas around the world.

Sea turtles spend nearly all their lives in the ocean. Only when she lays her eggs does the female sea turtle visit the beach. In late spring, the female turtle digs a hole in the sand. Then she lays 100 to 200 eggs in the hole. The eggs look like white Ping-Pong balls. She smooths the sand over the eggs with her flippers and heavy body. Then she slowly makes her way back to the sea.

When the baby turtles hatch, they struggle to push themselves up through the sand. They were born knowing that they must go to the sea. The babies are tiny, and the sea may be far from their nest; many dangers stand in their way. Crabs, birds, and other animals eat these tender young turtles. Out of the hundreds of turtles that leave a nest, only a few make it out to the sea.

The wings of a ray ripple and flutter as the ray "flies" through the water.

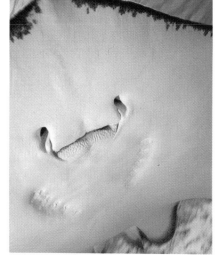

A ray's mouth is on its underside. Rays have broad, flat teeth made for crunching up shellfish.

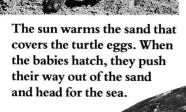

The sun warms the sand that covers the turtle eggs. When the babies hatch, they push their way out of the sand and head for the sea.

30

Whales live in the ocean, too. They swim, hunt, and breed in the water. Nevertheless, they are not fish. Whales are mammals: They are warm-blooded and breathe air with lungs instead of gills.

There are more than 75 different kinds of whales. They are divided into two groups depending on the way they catch their food. Whales that have teeth and that hunt are called "toothed whales." The other kinds are "baleen whales." Baleen whales hunt for food and sift plankton—krill and other small drifting animals—through baleen plates in their mouths.

This humpback whale (left) is a baleen whale. The killer whale (right) is a toothed whale.

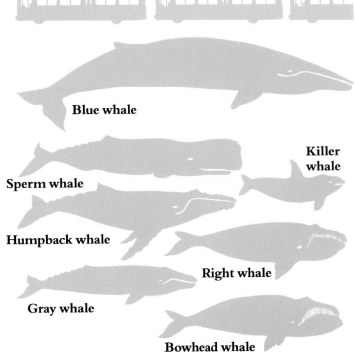

Blue whale

Killer whale

Sperm whale

Humpback whale

Right whale

Gray whale

Bowhead whale

The blue whale is the largest animal that has ever lived on earth. It is about as long as two and one-half school buses lined up end to end!

Baleen plates hang from the whale's upper jaw. They look like stiff bristles on a brush. The whale takes on a huge mouthful of seawater that contains millions of tiny animals. Next, it lowers its baleen plates without closing its whole mouth—like closing your teeth, but leaving your lips apart. Then, the whale uses its tongue to push the water back out through the baleen. The krill and other plankton are strained by the baleen and stay in the whale's mouth. The whale swallows the plankton and opens for another mouthful of water.

Dolphins and porpoises are toothed whales. Like all dolphins and porpoises, these spotted dolphins hunt in groups to round up prey.

THE ABYSS

is the deepest part of the sea. It is completely dark and very cold. At depths below 3,000 feet, the water pressure is great and the water itself is very, very still. There is life down here, though, and the animals have developed some odd ways of surviving.

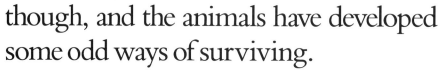

Many animals that live in the deep ocean have brittle skeletons or no skeletons at all. These wisps of animals could not withstand the moving waters above them. Many animals in the abyss are small, but some grow to be giants in the still, black water.

Some sea creatures have lost their need for sight. They use their other senses to help them find food. Some animals have huge eyes that gather any light nearby, for many animals here produce their own light.

Anglerfish like these wear a glowing "fishing lure" that dangles in front of their mouths. A fish that is drawn to the lure will probably be eaten.

Deep-sea creatures have different ways of surviving in the total darkness.

Lanternfish

The hatchetfish has big eyes on top of its head. Its eyes can concentrate dim light and help it see prey overhead.

In the deep, dark ocean, a faint light flickers. A fish swims toward it. Suddenly, WHOOSH! the fish disappears! What happened?

The light came from the anglerfish. This fish is about five inches long and has what looks like a fishing pole fastened to its forehead! The tip of the "pole" holds bacteria that glow. The light acts as bait to attract other fish to the anglerfish's mouth. When a fish swims near, the anglerfish opens wide and swallows.

The deep sea sparks and winks with lights. The creatures that make their own light are called *bioluminescent*. On land, the fireflies seen on a summer evening are bioluminescent. Bioluminescent light comes from chemicals in an animal's body.

A full-grown lanternfish is only about two inches long, from jaw to tail. But in spite of its size, it may have as many as 100 lights on its body! There are 32 lights on each of its sides, and more on its head, back, and tail.

These lights are not strong enough to light the darkness. They do help the lanternfish see other lanternfish, though. They can all swim together for protection. If an enemy comes near, the lanternfish put out their lights so they can't be seen. Food is scarce in the deep ocean. At night, lanternfish swim to shallower waters to feed.

The scaly dragonfish grows to be about 10 inches long. Nearly all dragonfish have a whisker, called a "barbel," attached to the chin. This barbel may be five times longer than the fish itself. It often has one or more lights that give off a faint glow.

Viperfish dangle a glowing lure in front of their mouth to attract prey. This deep-sea fish can unhinge its jaw to eat larger fish. Since food is scarce in the abyss, a meal must sometimes last a long time. Viperfish sometimes swim up toward the surface where food is more plentiful. The fierce-looking viperfish will grow to be only 12 inches long or less.

The bottom of the deep sea is made of ooze. The ooze is millions of years worth of dead plants and animals that have floated down and settled in layers. Most creatures on the sea floor are scavengers. They feel their way along the bottom, finding food as it drifts down. Some animals burrow into the ooze. Still others are rooted in it, like plants rooted in the soil.

The tripod fish can rest on the soft ooze without sinking. It has three long fins that support the fish, like a tripod holds a camera. When prey swims near, the tripod fish leaps from its resting place to snatch it.

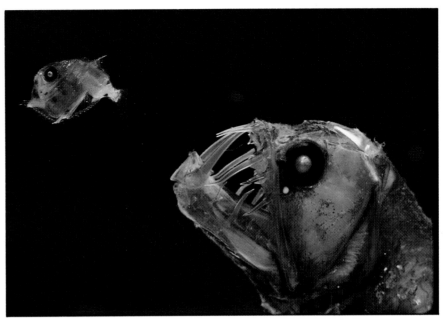

The jaws of the viperfish unhinge so that it can eat large prey.

Food is scarce in the abyss. Fish must be able to eat whatever they find, even if it is larger than themselves.

Dragonfish

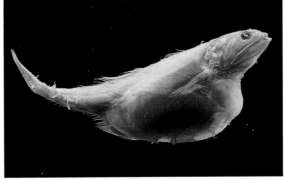

This black swallower's (left) stomach stretches to hold lots of food. The fierce-looking fangtooth (right) can catch prey that is much larger than itself.

35

SURVIVAL IN THE SEA

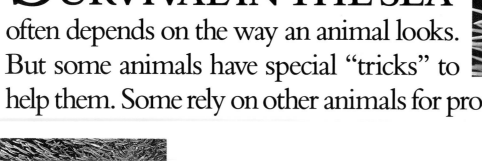

often depends on the way an animal looks. But some animals have special "tricks" to help them. Some rely on other animals for protection.

Many fish swim in schools, for there is safety in numbers. Some animals, like the lionfish, wear colors that say, "Beware! I'm poisonous!" Some wear protection, like spines, shells, or stingers. Still, the most common defense is to swim away from danger *fast!*

A fish has plenty of enemies in the sea, but there are some "friendships," too. Like the anemone and anemonefish, some animals are partners and help each other to find food and survive.

There are many strange relationships under the sea. Some animals form partnerships with other kinds of creatures. They help each other to find food, shelter, and protection. This partnership is called *symbiosis*.

The anemonefish can swim among the tentacles of a sea anemone without being stung. Scientists are not sure why the anemonefish won't be stung when all others will. It may be because a mucus coating on the fish's body protects it. Scientists think the anemonefish brings food to the anemone and eats the leftovers itself. The anemone protects the anemonefish nestled in its arms—most fish know not to come too close.

The brightly colored clown anemonefish (above) may attract predators to its host anemone. Instead of *having* dinner, the predator *is* dinner —to the stinging anemone.

Anemonefish, like this skunk clown (right), live in family groups with an anemone. The female lays eggs and the male keeps them clean by fanning them with his fins.

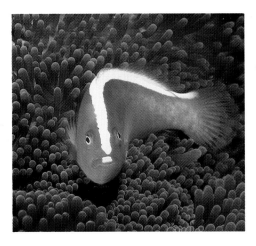

Some sea anemones hitch a ride on a hermit crab or boxer crab. Fastened to the crab's shell, they make it difficult to see the crab. If an enemy of the crab comes near, the anemones sting it with their tentacles. The sting drives away large animals and may kill small ones. What does the crab do for the anemones? Besides providing a home and transportation, the crab furnishes the anemones with its leftovers.

Sometimes a fish needs cleaning but cannot handle the job itself. Several kinds of small fish—wrasses and gobies—offer cleaning services for larger fish. These little helpers eat bits of dead skin and parasites off the bodies of their "customers." This cleaning service helps both fish. The cleaners get a meal and the large fish will stay healthy.

Neon goby

The wrasse and the goby will even serve customers that would normally eat a small fish. But a big fish rarely eats the wrasse or goby—even if the cleaner were to swim into its mouth! This is exactly what the goby does, too. The goby removes food from the teeth of the grouper. The goby gets a meal, and the grouper gets a healthy mouth.

These big fish know the cleaners by their colors and by the way they swim. The cleaner wrasse wears bold stripes and rocks side to side as it swims. Customers will line up for a cleaning by the wrasse. A wrasse may clean hundreds of fish a day!

Some gobies serve as "seeing-eye fish" for a kind of blind shrimp. The shrimp digs a burrow in the sea floor and shares it with the goby. The shrimp will fish for food just outside the hole. If danger threatens, the goby wiggles its body, and the shrimp feels the wiggle. Both the shrimp and the goby quickly disappear down the hole to safety!

This cleaner shrimp (left) may signal that it is ready to clean fish by rocking back and forth and whipping its long, white antennae. Even predators will not eat the shrimp while it is cleaning.

The yellowheaded wrasse (below) not only helps other animals by cleaning, but it also gets a meal in the process!

Cleaner fish and shrimp are able to swim safely into a predator's mouth to clean— their customers need cleaning more than they need a meal.

This grouper will be a much healthier fish when the gobies finish the cleaning job!

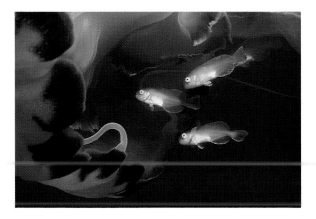

Like the Portuguese man-of-war and the shepherdfish, some jellyfish have a partnership with fish they might normally eat. These medusa fish are protected by the jellyfish. They lure other fish into the jellyfish's tentacles.

The Portuguese man-of-war and the shepherdfish have a strange partnership, too. The Portuguese man-of-war floats at the top of the water, its "float" acting as a sail. Under the float, hanging far down in the water are dozens of stinging tentacles. Some of the tentacles may be 100 feet long. Few fish will survive the sting of the Portuguese man-of-war. But the small shepherdfish actually makes its home in the tangle. The shepherdfish is not hurt at all! It lures other fish into the tentacles for the man-of-war to eat and then feeds on the leftover bits of food. Without its protector, the shepherdfish would be easy prey for bigger fish.

Remoras "hitch" rides on rays and sharks. These remoras may eat bits of food that this manta ray leaves behind.

This remora is attached to a nurse shark (below).

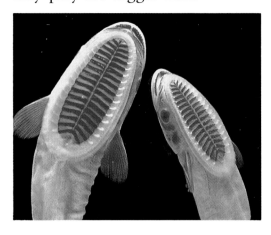

The remora, or shark sucker, hitchhikes on sharks. The remora is long and thin, with a suction cup on its head (above). The remora fastens itself onto a shark for a free ride. Sometimes, the remora gets a free meal, too. When the shark eats, the remora get the scraps that fall from the shark's jaws. The remora also attaches itself to sea turtles, swordfish, rays, and some whales.

Some sea creatures fool their enemies by wearing disguises. Others wear the colors or patterns of their surroundings. Both of these "tricks" are called *camouflage*.

As the decorator crab (above) crawls across the ocean floor, it picks up pieces of seaweed and puts it on its body. It may even pick up sponges or anemones to wear. Can you see the crab in this picture? Its enemies can't see it either.

The octopus is a master of disguise. If the ocean floor on which it is resting is brown, the octopus turns brown. If it is swimming through seaweed, the octopus turns seaweed-green. It may turn coral red, too. Some kinds of octopus can even be several colors at once!

When a ray comes to rest on the ocean floor, it waves its "wings" to stir up the sand around it. The sand settles and lightly covers the ray's body. Hidden like this, the ray will wait for a meal to swim by.

Flounder and other flatfish are experts at disguising themselves against the ocean floor. Rather than arrange the sand over them, they change their skin to match the bottom. They may even become spotted to match a pebbly ocean floor.

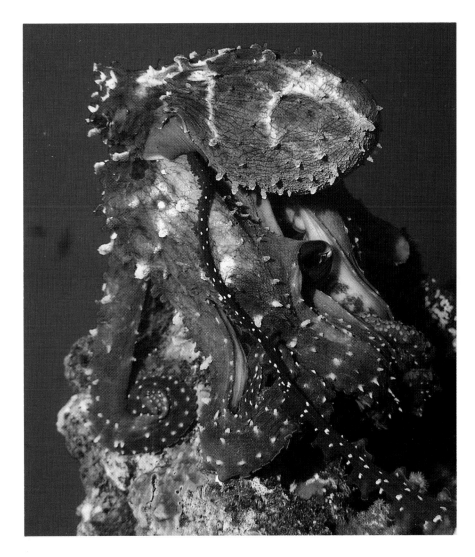

An octopus can change both its color and its skin texture to hide. It can make its skin look like rock!

This stingray (left) hides in the sand and awaits its next meal. The flatfish (right) hides so it will not be a meal. Can you see it against the pebbly floor?

41

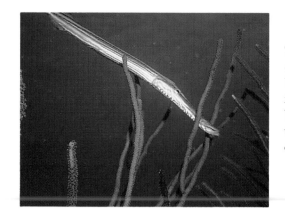

The trumpetfish (left) often hangs among branching coral and waits for a small fish to swim by. To its enemies, the trumpetfish looks like one of the coral branches.

The long, slender trumpetfish hangs in the water among soft coral branches. Like the octopus, it can change color to match its hiding spot. Safe from predators, the trumpetfish eats small fish and plankton drifting by.

The lionfish's coloring warns predators to stay away!

Sea urchins are good examples of animals that defend themselves with spines—they are covered with them. Only a few animals will try to eat an urchin. The crown-of-thorns sea star (above) is another spiny animal. It has short, sharp spines along each of its five arms. These spines can cause a painful wound. The porcupine fish has spines that lay flat against its body until the fish is in danger. If danger nears, the porcupine fish quickly takes in water and makes itself bigger. Now the spines stick out all over. Few fish would want a mouthful of this!

The porcupine fish protects itself by quickly sucking water into its body. This makes its spines stick out straight (left). An "un-puffed" porcupine fish's spines lie almost flat against its skin (above).

Some sea creatures are poisonous or stinging. Some fish, like the lionfish, wear warning signs—colors or spines—to caution others to stay away. If someone or something were to get too close to the lionfish, they would receive a painful jab from a poisonous spine.

A jellyfish has no brain and does not move quickly. It protects and feeds itself by using its stinging tentacles.

A bristleworm (above) looks like a furry caterpillar. The "fur" is really hollow needles that can be used to inject a painful poison.

Many kinds of scorpionfish live on the ocean floor and have poisonous spines on their top fins. The most deadly kind of scorpionfish is the stonefish. It has 13 spines along its back. The spines are like hollow needles, each with a poison sac. The stonefish's shape and color help it blend with rocks on the floor. It will stay very still there. To step on the stonefish would be quite painful—perhaps even deadly.

Jellyfish, however, do not "advertise" their stinging tentacles. Instead, the jellyfish drifts through the water, hanging its stinging tentacles down in hopes that prey will swim into them. When a jellyfish brushes against a fish or another animal swimming by, the tentacles paralyze the victim so it cannot swim away. Then the jellyfish pulls its tentacles and the prey up to its mouth on the underside of its body.

The scorpionfish (above left) and the stonefish (below left) both have poisonous spines on their backs.

Fire coral (right) is not coral at all. It is a relative of the Portuguese man-of-war. If you were to touch it, you would get some painful burning stings.

GLOSSARY

Abalone (AB-uh-LOH-nee): A large sea snail valued for its shell and meat.

Abyss (uh-BISS): The deepest, darkest part of the ocean.

Algae (AL-jee): Ocean seaweeds and simple fresh water plants able to use the sun's energy to make food.

Anemone (uh-NEM-uh-nee): A soft, sac-shaped animal with stinging tentacles around its mouth, which help it catch small animals for food.

Atmosphere (AT-moss-feer): All of the air, moisture, and dust surrounding a planet.

Baleen (buh-LEEN): Fringed plates that hang down from the upper jaw of some whales. Baleen strains krill and small fish from the water for the whale to swallow.

Bioluminescent (by-oh-loo-mih-NESS-ent): The word used to describe fish and other living things that create their own light.

Camouflage (KAM-oh-flahj): Colors and patterns that help an animal hide in nature.

Cleaner Fish: A small fish that often acts as a cleaning partner for larger fish.

Community: A group of plants and animals living in the same area.

Crustacean (kruhs-TAY-shun): An animal that lives in water and has a hard shell and antennae. Shrimps, lobsters, and crabs are some crustaceans.

Fossil (FAHS-uhl): A trace of a plant or animal preserved in rock or sediment after many years.

Frond (frahnd): The branch of a seaweed. It is composed of a stemlike stipe and leaflike blades.

Gills: The breathing organs of fish, snails, and nudibranchs.

Habitat (HAB-uh-tat): Where a plant or animal lives; the special kind of environment it needs to survive.

Holdfast: The rootlike base of a seaweed that anchors it to rocks or other surfaces.

Krill (kril): Shrimplike crustaceans that are the main food of most baleen whales.

Mollusk (MAH-lusk): A soft-bodied animal often surrounded by a hard shell, such as snails, clams, and oysters.

Nudibranch (NOOD-uh-brahnk): A generally soft-bodied "sea slug."

Paralyze (PAIR-uh-lyz): To make prey inactive so that it may be eaten.

Parasite (PAIR-uh-syt): A plant or animal that lives on or in a "host" plant or animal. A parasite can harm or kill its host.

Plankton (PLANK-tuhn): Plants or animals, often very small, that drift in the ocean.

Polyp (PAHL-up): A simple sac-shaped animal with a mouth—and usually tentacles—at one end.

Predator (PRED-uh-tor): Any animal that catches, kills, and eats other animals.

Prey (pray): The animals that are eaten by predators.

Reef: An underwater ridge built by the skeletons of hard corals or rocks.

Remora (ruh-MOR-uh): A fish that uses the suction cup on its head to stick to larger fish, hitching rides on them and eating scraps of their food.

Scavenger (SCAV-en-jer): An animal that feeds on dead or discarded things, rather than catching live prey.

Sponge (spunj): A sea animal with a soft skeleton that is full of holes. Sponges come in all sizes, shapes, and colors.

Symbiosis (sim-bee-OH-sis): A give-and-take relationship between different kinds of living things in which both creatures benefit.

Tentacle (TENT-uh-kuhl): An armlike part of an animal, usually for feeding.

Tropical (TROP-ih-kuhl): A word that describes a region that is warm all year because it is near the equator.